Starfish

TO: OTTO

What a blessed boy you are Otto, to have so many loving arms to hold you! I love that my book will be added to your collection!

xoxo

Pat Gleichauf

PATRICIA GLEICHAUF

ILLUSTRATED BY

SHARI HOLCOMB

Shari Holcomb

PAGE PUBLISHING, INC.
New York, NY

First originally published by Page Publishing, Inc. 2018

ISBN 978-1-64298-805-5 (Paperback)
ISBN 978-1-64298-806-2 (Hardcover)
ISBN 978-1-64298-807-9 (Digital)

Printed in the United States of America

Starfish Gazing is dedicated to the many family members and friends who made this book possible with their tremendous support of *Horses of the Sea*.

To you the parent, grandparent, aunt, uncle, cousin, niece, nephew, and friend who bought *Horses of the Sea* for a little person in your life or just for yourself. There is not enough space on this page to list all of your names. Please know that your name is etched in my forever grateful heart. This one is for *you*! xoxo

If you gaze into the sea,

you might see starfish 1, 2, 3.

**You won't have to search
the nighttime sky**

to see stars in the
water floating by.

A starfish is a saltwater animal
that is shaped like a star.

**They are found in every ocean,
very near and very far.**

They are called starfish, but they
are not fish. They cannot swim.

They have no spine.
They have no fins.

Most starfish have five arms.
Some have many more.

There are different types of starfish found on every distant shore.

Each arm has a tiny eyespot
on its tip for sight.

Not to see color, only daytime from night.

Starfish can lose an arm while running from danger. If this happens, they need not fear.

Their arm will grow completely back within the coming year!

Their skin helps protect them. It
is a thick and prickly covering.

It keeps their space much safer
when predators are hovering.

Starfish have hundreds of tiny tube feet that they use for locomotion.

With them they can crawl along
the bottom of the ocean.

Tube feet look like suction cups that also help them grip.

When they are climbing over rocks,
tube feet help them not to slip.

Starfish wash ashore with the tide.
They often land on their dorsal side.

When they land upside down,
they simply do a somersault
to turn themselves around.

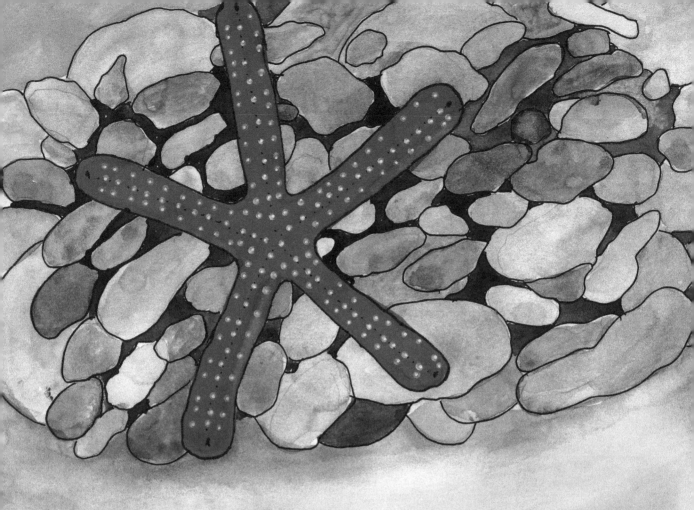

They explore rocks and tide pools, searching for meat.

Mussels, clams, and oysters are
their favorite foods to eat.

Their colors are brilliant, purple, red, orange, green, and blue.

**Starfish blend with ocean colors
to keep safely out of view.**

**The beauty of starfish
is for all to see.**

A gift from the ocean for you and for me!

ABOUT THE AUTHOR

Pat "Anthony" Gleichauf has always loved to write stories for children. Recently retired from a career in research, she now has time to focus on writing. *Starfish Gazing* is her second book in a series about unusual sea creatures. Pat grew up in Binghamton, New York, one of six children. She now lives in Upstate New York with her husband, Jack. They raised their two children in Avon, New York and have five grandchildren, who are the loves of their life. Her first book in the series, *Horses of the Sea*, was awarded a gold metal in the 2018 Florida Authors and Publishers Association (FAPA) President's Awards.

ABOUT THE ILLUSTRATOR

Shari "Knight Williams" Holcomb grew up in Gladwin, Michigan. After high school, she moved to Palmer, Alaska, where she married, raised a daughter, and resided for thirty-two years. During that time, she completed BFA in drawing from the University of Alaska and later an MA in art history from Savannah College of Art and Design in Georgia. Shari taught art in the Alaska college system and in her studio for many years. Returning to Michigan in 2005, she taught at Mid Michigan Community College. Now remarried and retired, Shari spends summers in Gladwin and winters in Venice, Florida.

CPSIA information can be obtained
at www.ICGtesting.com
Printed in the USA
BVHW020725301018
531056BV00002B/4/P